GOD'S HOUSE
Welcome Home

WRITTEN BY **SARAH SIM**   ILLUSTRATED BY **ABBIE REUSS**

God's House: Welcome Home by Sarah Sim

Copyright © 2022

All rights reserved.

ISBN: 978-1-7781300-0-7

Illustrated by Abbie Reuss

Dedication

To my Heavenly Daddy who always shows up, trades up and never gives up.
Thank You for all You are and all You do. It's all about You; to Your glory alone.

To my amazing husband who releases me into ministry;
your love and sacrifice enables and inspires me to fulfill my destiny.
Thank you for helping me help others find freedom
so that they, too, may truly know the love of their Father.

To a special client who revealed to me a deeper understanding of the love of the Father and
showed me undeniable proof that He always meets us right where we are,
tailor made encounters for each of His beloved children.
There really are no wrong answers and it's always the right path
to journey when Holy Spirit is the Guide.
No matter where you go in life, I pray that you always take Home with you.

When I was a kid, summer time was the best! Every day my friends and I rode our bikes together down the country roads that crisscrossed through the trees. When we were quiet, feeling the rushing wind cool our faces in competition with the sun's rays to warm us, the sound of birds would fill our ears and animals would poke their faces out from between the trees to stare at us as we whizzed by. Other days, we'd be laughing and shouting so much the world would go silent and motionless as we disrupted the lives of all the forest creatures.

One day as the sun stood high in the sky, empty stomachs began to tell us it was noon. My friends dropped away one by one as we passed their homes, and I soon found myself alone as I rode my bike in search of my own lunch.

I'm not really sure how it happened; I must have hit a rock or maybe a hole or something. All I know is I was laying in a heap, blood on my arm and forehead and more pain than I had ever known before coming from my ankle. My bike was destroyed as the front wheel was broken off and the forks bent beyond repair. My riding shoe was still clipped in to the bent and twisted pedal, explaining the pain in my ankle.

My broken ankle and bike slipped from the front of my mind as I became all too aware that I was alone. There were no houses in sight, not even my own, and all the animals and birds had slipped silently away. I had been way too busy for God that summer. My friends and I had been having fun, sometimes choosing to do things that I knew God wouldn't want me to do . . . My sinful choices made me feel far away from God, but I knew I needed Him now. I felt alone and hurt so in my desperation I decided to look for God.

"God, I need you!" I cried out. My stomach turned as the pain pushed its way back to mind, demanding my full attention. The world began to spin as the sounds of nature once again filled my ears and whirled into one indistinguishable sound. Everything spun faster and faster and the trees melted away in a blur . . . .

I found myself in a field with a single tree in front of me . . . my tree; I just knew it was mine. As wide as it was tall, big green leaves danced in the breeze, playing peek-a-boo with the beautiful red fruit that hung heavy from its many branches. A brilliant white building on the edge of the field revealed itself when a huge gust of wind bent my tree low to the ground. The single doorway to the building was small and the door was swung open wide. I just knew I was looking at God's house and I could tell He was inside, but I could not get in through that open doorway. More than the creek that ran between the tree and the building prevented me from going inside.

To my surprise my friend came out through the doorway. She had chosen to stop hanging out with us earlier that summer and hurt my feelings badly when she left our group. I could tell that God wanted me to forgive her.

"God, I choose to forgive my friend for all the ways she hurt my feelings and for leaving me behind without explaining why or ever calling to say hello. Jesus, please forgive me for ever believing You would treat me the same way she did. You will never choose to stop being my friend." A very small smile crept across my face as forgiveness washed over me.

God sent my dad out of His house next, but he didn't come over to me. My dad headed around the corner of God's house, beckoning for me to follow. He indicated that he wanted to show me something. But no matter how hard I tried, I could not go behind the house; something just prevented me. Soon my dad came around the corner of the house and started out across the field, entering the woods on the far side. Running across the field, I tried my best but could not find the path my dad had taken.

Growing up, my dad and I spent many days walking through the woods together, admiring all that God had made. He would stoop down and pick up something that had caught his attention and use it to teach me something wonderful about God and how much care He took in creating everything, especially me. I just wanted him to be able to show me that God still cared for me. It made me feel so sad and frustrated that I couldn't go with him into the woods.

Then suddenly I understood what God was trying to help me to know about my relationship with my dad. So I prayed, "God, I choose to forgive my dad for being unable to lead me in a way that I can understand. My sad heart has lied to me and told me that there's no place for me in our family, that he doesn't understand me or love me and that he can't help me navigate this world. And worse, it told me that You don't know how to lead me so that I can really follow You. Please forgive me. I give these lies to You so that I can know Your truth."

When I finished praying I turned away from the woods and saw my dad, my friend and my mom all standing near my tree. Surprised to see him over there, I ran back to be with him. Stopping to look at my tree, I picked a piece of its fruit to give to my mom. As soon as I did, the once beautiful, red fruit turned rotten. Bewildered, I looked to her for answers, but quickly saw that she was just as sad and confused as me. So God told me what I needed to do.

"God, I choose to forgive my mom for not being able to comfort and guide me when I felt so abandoned. I turned my back on all the good I had been taught and chose to go my own way. Holy Spirit, please forgive me for thinking You weren't there for me either. Thank you for always being there for me, even when I couldn't see that You were."

I looked around at the meadow, my tree, God's house... I could tell something wasn't quite right. The colours had changed; they were too dark and muted. God nudged my heart to look around and I found a pair of sunglasses sitting on a rock.

I walked over to them and realized that somehow the wrong glasses were already on my face, causing me to be unable to see the world for what it is. Taking these glasses off, I said, "God, my wounded heart has caused me to see the world through these glasses; they have tainted my view of everything and everyone. I have made wrong assumptions and taken offense because I could not see clearly what was happening, using this filter of hurt to interpret my world. I am being lied to by these glasses and I didn't even know I was wearing them."

I took them off and handed them up to God. He told me the sunglasses were for me and I should put them on. Looking through these sunglasses that had been waiting there for me changed everything. The world was brightly coloured and vibrant again; you could almost see joy in its beauty. "Thank You, God, for these new lenses to see the world through. I just know that I'm going to be able to see everything differently now and it is going to be so good!"

Looking out at the rightly coloured world, no one else spoke, and I stood in my quiet field and listened to the creek bubble along. The breeze caressed my skin and tussled my hair. "What now God, is there someone else I need to forgive? Oh . . ." His words resonated in my heart and convicted me. "God, I have done so many bad things that I am really sorry I did. Please forgive me. I have this big weight of Guilt that I don't want to carry anymore. I give Guilt to You now. What do You have for me?" Father God was quick to forgive me. But more than that, He took Guilt from my hands and gave me hope in exchange.

As I thought about my new gift of hope, I was happy to see my grandma come out of God's house with a picnic basket in her hand. She laid out a red and white checkered blanket beside the happy creek and motioned for me to sit with her. She smiled warmly at me and opened her basket. To my surprise, she pulled out some of my fruit; it was still red and beautiful. She had saved some before the rest had rotted. She helped me see that she, too, had had a part to play in life being hard for me from her generational line, and somehow I knew in my heart that God wanted me to forgive her for that.

"God, I choose to forgive my grandma and all the generations before her. They opened a door to Rejection in my life. Heal the root of my rejection that I might bear good fruit again. Please forgive me for believing more lies about You, Holy Spirit. I give all the sin and lies to You; I want only to live in Your truth."

That's when God called to me from inside His house and told me I was ready to come in. In the center of the foyer was God's tree enrobed in a single beam of light. My grandpa emerged from the darkness that enveloped the vast emptiness of the rest of the room and pulled my attention away from God's tree. As I turned to face him, God whispered to my heart that I needed to forgive him too, but like Grandma, not just him.

"God, I choose to forgive my grandpa and all the generations before him for opening a door of sin in my life. I give the Impurity that has come through his line to You. What do You have for me in exchange?" When I handed Impurity to Him, the most beautiful purple, royal cloak appeared on my shoulders.

I stared at my new cloak. It was thick and warm and yet made me feel so light. "That can't stay in My house," I heard God whisper. My eyes flew open wide as I knew exactly what He was talking about; up until then I had forgotten all about the day I was having and I felt embarrassed by what was still in my pocket. The drugs in my pocket were not the first ones given to me by my friends; we had been doing drugs together for a while, but that quickly turned into wanting to do them when I was home alone too. I didn't hesitate to hand them to God.

"Please forgive me for partnering with Addiction and using drugs as a false protector to hide from my fears, insecurities and wrong belief that I am not lovable. I hand Addiction to You. What do You have for me in exchange?" The drugs disappeared and a loaf of bread manifested in my hands.

I turned to look once again at the tree in the big empty room, thinking how different it looked from my fruit tree, so filled with perpetual life. There was no denying I had made choices to sin because I wanted to punish God, my family and myself for how misunderstood and alone I felt. I had forgiven, but hadn't yet broken off my partnership with Rebellion.

"God, please forgive me for choosing to do the things I knew were not what I should be doing. I partnered with Rebellion and turned away from You. I am sorry. I give Rebellion to You; please take it. What do You have for me in exchange?"

God gave me the key to His house. In that moment, God wanted me to know from Him how much He cares, not a lesson from someone else; God Himself was telling me. He does care for the animals and birds. He sees the fields and dresses them beautifully with flowers. And He loves me . . . me . . . . He loves me.

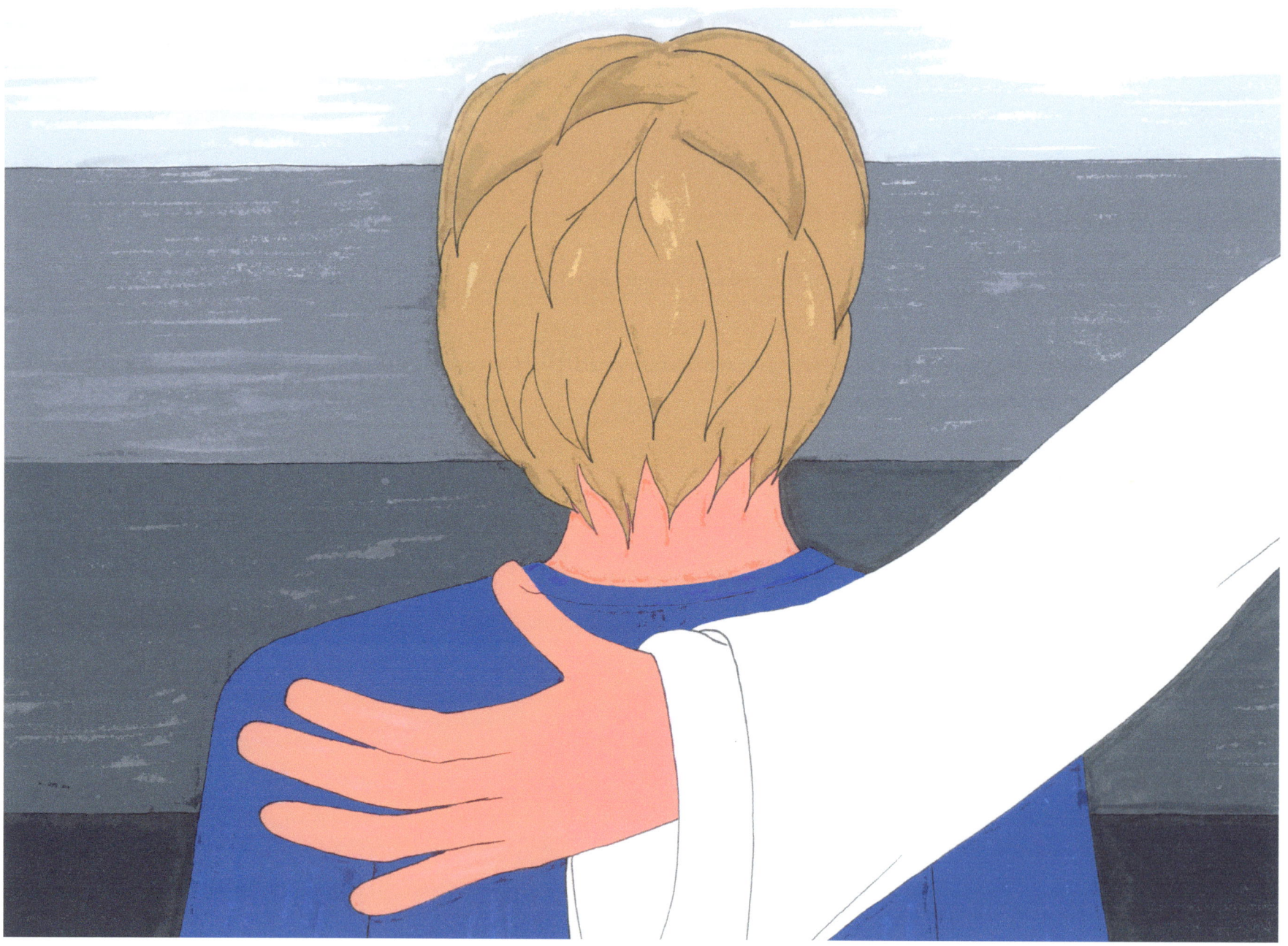

God put His arm around me and showed me to my room. As we walked up the stairs to my new room, I began to understand that He didn't just give me the key to His house; He gave me the key to my house. He was happy to have me home with Him again, and it felt so amazing to be there.

I opened my eyes to see my mom over me, calling my name. Gently she bound a stick to my ankle and untied my shoe to free me from the twisted metal bike. She helped me to the back seat of our family car and drove me to the hospital. Her voice sounded incessantly in my ears, but I could not hear her words. Mom had wrapped a purple blanket around me. A sandwich sat on the seat next to me with a gleaming red apple sitting on the napkin beside it. My house key must have fallen out of my pocket and mom, having seen its glint in the sunlight, picked it up and tossed it on the seat too. I quickly checked my pocket, horrified that mom might have found the drugs . . . but they were gone and she never mentioned them.

At the hospital I sat in confusion, trying to make sense of all I knew had happened with God. "God, are You really there? Did I really go to Your house?" The words spilled out in a whispered cry as I ached to know that I hadn't just dreamt it all. It was real. It had to be. God really does love me and He gave me a room in His house. He forgave me as I forgave others and gave me amazing gifts.

"The world you see with your eyes is an echo of what I am doing. Those are My gifts for you to use now, a reminder of all the good work we did." These words washed over my heart as a tear ran down my cheek.

Mom assured me that the pain would lessen soon. I smiled and put my head on her shoulder like I used to when I was younger and whispered, "I love you, mom." I told her and dad all about my day with God. They cried with me and dad held mom and me for a long time.

The temptation to go back to my old life was strong. I didn't have any friends that knew God and I didn't know yet how to do life without them. My friends would leave me alone for short times, but would always come back and invite me to do something. Everything began to feel hard and I felt like I couldn't fight the demons that were coming against me, drawing me back. I just wanted to be with my friends again, doing whatever they were doing. I didn't want to be confused, sad and alone, and I couldn't fight anymore. All of that made me forget about how great it was to be living in my new house with God. So one day, I left with them. I'm not sure that I really wanted to go; I just didn't know how to stay.

I hadn't left for very long before I knew I needed desperately to get back inside God's house. All that had looked so fun and inviting proved to be empty and didn't make me feel better. In fact I felt even more lonely and sad while hanging out with my friends, who just didn't understand my journey, than I had felt at home alone. I couldn't see God's house anymore in my mind. All I could see now was the red, wooden door with the gold handle. But now, the door was shut. I thought that meant that I wasn't allowed back inside…

Alone, I lay down on the soft green grass under a small tree in our backyard one cool fall day. Watching the light of the sun waltz through the leaves, I thought of that day weeks before when God showed me my tree. I wondered about its fruit; was the tree alive at all? My eyes grew heavy as I stared at the dancing light. "Are You there?" I murmured as the world faded away in a wash of greens.

I was standing in a place I had never been before. I turned around and saw my same friend standing a little ways away from me. Seeing her this time was just as painful as the last, so I knew I had more to forgive.

"God, she hurt me so badly. I really thought we would be friends forever and now she doesn't want to be my friend at all. Even still she refuses to let me back in her life. Jesus, forgive me for thinking that You would one day choose to no longer be my friend. I'm sorry I have chosen to let my sadness turn to bitterness. I don't want to be bitter anymore. I hand Bitterness to You."

God showed me that it wasn't my fault she couldn't be my friend now. She had her own hurts that made her too scared to be in a friendship; it was her fear that made her run away. I asked Him if I believed a lie and He gave me a well worn pair of hiking boots. I didn't really understand what the boots were for or what they meant, but as I set them on the ground beside me, I realized Bitterness was gone. With Bitterness gone, I became aware of some anger growing in my heart; I didn't want it anymore either. So I handed Anger to God too. He took Anger from me and handed me a ladybug.

"I'm tired, God. I don't want to chase Your mysteries. I don't want to . . . anything." With a sigh I put the ladybug down. Sitting on a huge rock, feeling exhausted from confusion and disappointment, I thought I didn't even want to look for God's house anymore.

As I sat on that rock, I could see people rushing past me like a streak of lightning. Like a blur they followed a path that had escaped my notice as it wound past my rock and to the door of God's house. I'm not sure when the door showed up, but it wasn't far from me and the path looked easy to walk. The people would run by and slip through the door in a bright flash of light that came from inside. So much light around me, so much excitement, but I was too worn out from my journey to go see for myself.

A new friend came along slowly and deliberately. "Proclaim peace and happiness; speak destiny and life... That feels like a funny thing to say," she said with a warm smile, looking, really looking at me. "Why would God ask me to say that to you?"

I didn't know what those words were supposed to mean. I remained motionless on my rock feeling somehow better but still confused and tired. She didn't stop looking intently at me for a few minutes, clearly unwilling to let it go. She wanted to understand why God had sent her to me.

"Oh! I see... You have some extra bags that are weighing you down." She walked over to me and took four big bags from my back that I somehow hadn't realized were there. The bags had labels on them: "Turmoil," "Sorrow," "Hopelessness," and "Death." She broke the cords that tied them to me. The bags weighing me down were the opposite of the words God wanted me to know, "Peace," "Happiness," "Destiny," and "Life." Once the bags were on the ground, she told me to get up and open the door, that it would be easy for me to go there now.

Taking a deep breath, I slowly got up and walked over to the door. Suddenly the world around me became clearer and I could see that the red door was in the side of the ladybug God had given to me.

In my heart I heard Him whisper, "I gave you something you believed was really small and insignificant; it was only the beginning of something really big! Don't give up hope. I am always working and I always give you everything you need . . . even when you can't see that yet."

He had freely handed me His house before I even asked for it; He knew why I had come. My heart was just too hurt to understand that. Now that I was ready, I easily opened the red door. The bright light shone strong on my face, blinding me for a moment. I slowly blinked and stepped inside.

Mountains were all around me, and before me was a field of long, green grass dappled with flowers, and best of all, God was everywhere. I slipped my feet into the boots God had given me. They were a perfect fit and broken in just right. With Bitterness gone, I was free to walk this new journey with God. I walked through the meadow to the cabin which rested against the crystal clear mountain lake. I breathed deep the mountain air, feeling alive again. I didn't have to look for God anymore; I was home.

I sat down on the porch next to Jesus and enjoyed His peaceful presence. I never wanted to leave. "There's something else you need," Jesus said, breaking through the quiet. "All of the sins you've committed and all the sins committed against you have wounded your soul. Let's get you cleaned up." He used His blood to wash me clean.

"There, now we can get you all healed up too." Jesus shone His glory light onto the wounds of my soul, cauterizing them and causing them to completely disappear. "You are not just forgiven, but healed from the wounds the sin created. You will find it much easier to stay with Me now that you don't have anything in common with your past sin and sadness anymore."

His words were spoken with such a warm smile that I knew deep in my soul they were true. He squeezed my shoulder and stayed close beside me. My heart overflowed with peace as I sat there with Jesus, the warm sun shining brightly on our faces. "Now what, Jesus?" was the question on my heart. I have learned that it's the second of two questions to ask Him every day. You see, I want to do whatever He tells me to, to follow wherever He leads, but I can't follow Him when I'm bound in my sin. To stay free, and to make new wounds on my soul impossible, I also ask Him every day, "Who do I need to forgive?"

Acknowledgments

Sarah Baer, the graphic artist who took all 30 of Abbie's amazing drawings and made them even more amazing, getting them publish ready for this book.

Ruth Klepel for her encouragement and support and ability to remember the details.

Maureen Sim for willingly editing this work and providing such valuable feedback.

Melinda Martin of Martin Publishing Services for taking all the pieces these beautiful women contributed and making it into a book that will touch lives for the Kingdom.

Thank you all!

About the Author
Sarah Sim

Passionately in love with Jesus, Sarah shares her life with her husband, Shawn on a hobby farm in rural Saskatchewan. Together they have been blessed with 3 sons, 5 daughters, a daughter-in-law and 1 grandchild and numerous bonus (foster) children. They co-founded Simply Whole to offer Spirit-led counseling, coaching and support to families, individuals and ministry leaders who long for spiritual freedom for themselves, their loved ones and congregations. Visit them at SimplyWhole.Today.

About the Illustrator
Abbie Reuss

Living enthusiastically for God, Abbie resides in Saskatoon, Saskatchewan, creatively touching the hearts of everyone she meets with the overflowing joy of the Lord and the boundless love of our amazing God.

Five Steps to Freedom through Forgiveness

Step 1: Who do I need to forgive?

It is exceptionally difficult to go through each day completely unoffended. Without realizing it, these offenses wound our soul and create conditions which are perfect for the enemy to plant a lie and gain a foothold in our lives. Matthew 18:21–35 tells us that unforgiveness imprisons us; living in an environment in which *we* are tortured. Ask Holy Spirit everyday, "Who do I need to forgive?"

Step 2: Choose forgiveness.

Now that you know who you need to forgive, you need to actually say it out loud. "I choose to forgive _____ for _____." Be sure you use the word *choose*. "Help me to," "I want to," etc. is not forgiving. Boldly make the choice to forgive and then forgive for *everything* Holy Spirit brings to mind. Luke 6:37 also shows us that forgiveness is for our own benefit, so that *we* can be forgiven.

Step 3: What lie was planted in me?

Ask, "What is the lie I am believing?" The father of lies is a devouring lion seeking to destroy. He is laying in wait to plant lies whenever the soil conditions are right. Wounded souls are fertile ground and his seeds will grow and distort our view of the world, making relationship increasingly difficult as a stronghold is established. If you cannot discern what the lie is, there's more to do in step 2; forgive specifically.

Step 4: What is Your truth?

"I renounce this lie and break off its power over me in Jesus' name. As I hand it to You, what is the truth You want me to know?" Hand God the lie and wait for Him to trade up as He always gives something amazing in return. This part is fun; there are no wrong answers from God. Holy Spirit may give you a word, Scripture, lyric, picture, feeling or color. Press in and let Him reveal the layered meaning behind His gift of truth.

Step 5: Prayers of Blessing

Luke 6:28 tells us to "bless those who curse you, pray for those who mistreat you." As we release blessing to those who have hurt us, something truly fantastic happens; we truly do find freedom through forgiveness! When we bless others, the Light of the World shines more brightly in our lives, giving us the victory over the darkness of sin and death. Then . . . see step 1 for more victory!

www.ingramcontent.com/pod-product-compliance
Lightning Source LLC
Chambersburg PA
CBHW042108090526

44590CB00005B/134